Tricky Thai Words

Grammar and Mini Reader

Tony J Richardson

Tricky Thai Words
Copyright © JiaHu Books 2015
First Published in Great Britain in 2015 by Jiahu Books – part of
Richardson-Prachai Solutions Ltd, 34 Egerton Gate, Milton Keynes,
MK5 7HH
ISBN: 978-1-78435-119-9

A CIP catalogue record for this book is available from the British
Library
Visit us at: jiahubooks.co.uk

INTRODUCTION

The main body of this book is set out in a simple and fairly self-explanatory way. The key words are listed in alphabetical order, and each word's meanings are listed roughly in order of frequency and importance. The sample sentences given aim to be as realistic as possible. This refers not only to the grammatical accuracy, but also that the tone and vocabulary is appropriate to the word under discussion. Therefore words which occur mainly in the written language will have example taken from newspapers and other written media while less formal words will tend to have examples from speech.

When it comes to translations, it should be noted that often tenses are not marked in Thai but need to be supplied in the English. The student should not expect to see every past tense marked with แล้ว and every future verb to be preceded by จะ as this simply does not happen in idiomatic Thai.

One concession has been made to simplicity is that the number of pronouns has been kept to a minimum. This can been done without impinging on the correct nature of most of the Thai sentences. The exception to this rule are the few instances of ราชาศัพท์ or royal language which necessitates the use of certain, extremely formal pronouns.

There is also a mini-reader of five newspaper style articles at the end of the book to provide the student with an opportunity to read some authentic Thai.

ก็

An adverb of extremely high frequency. It occurs between the subject and the verb when both expressed. It is translated variously as *then, so, consequently* and *also,* but in many cases it may be considered an emphatic particle and left untranslated.

ถ้ารายงานของคุณเห็นสมควรก็จะได้เสนอต่อไปยัง รัฐมนตรี

If your report is suitable *then* it will be submitted to the Minister.

พ่อทำงานที่โรงงานเสร็จแล้ว พ่อก็รับไปประชุมต่อ

As soon as he had finished work at the factory, father rushed to the meeting.

สาเหตุที่ต้องเป็นเช่นนี้ก็เพราะว่า

The reason why it should be like this is because...

ผมก็อยากจะไปกับคุณ

I want to go with you.

เมื่อไรก็ได้

any time, any time with

เอาไงก็เอากัน

Whatever you want.

กลาง

A noun meaning *middle* or *centre*. It has many idiomatic uses, some of which are illustrated below.

คณะกรรมการกลางของพรรค

The Central Committee of the Party

สงครามกลางเมือง

civil war (war inside the "city")

ชาติที่เป็นกลาง

a neutral nation (a nation which is "middle")

เขายืนอยู่กลางถนน

He stood in the middle of the road.

เขาทำงานทั้งกลางวันกลางคืน

He works day and night.

กว่า

Sign of the comparative containing the meaning of both *more* and *than*.

a) expressed

โตเกียวมีพลเมืองมากกว่าเมืองอื่นใดในโลก

Tokyo has a larger population than any other city in the world.

ผมอยากไปมากกว่าอยากอยู่ที่นี่

I would rather go than stay here.

b) implied

นี่ดีกว่ามาก

This is much better.

อย่าถามฉันเลยดีกว่า

It would be better not to ask me at all.

This last use is especially common.

ก่อน

Used:

a) adverbially (*first of all, previously*)

จะต้องเจรจากันเรื่องพม่าก่อน

It will be necessary to discuss the issue of Myanmar first of   all.

ผู้ที่ผมเคยเห็นมาก่อน

individuals whom I had seen before.

b) as a preposition (*before*)

ก่อนสงคราม

before the war

c) as a conjunction i.e. "*before*" in front of a verb. In this sense it is followed by ที่ subject จะ

ก่อนที่เราจะพิจารณาเรื่องนี้

Before we consider this matter

กัน

Suffixed to a verb this particle denotes reciprocality (*each other*), plurality (*together*) and occasionally, when the subject is unexpressed, the passive voice. It can be left untranslated. It can be seen as a variant

of **กับ** below; **กับ** becomes **กัน** when there is no following noun

phrase. See **ด้วย, เดียว, ร่วม** and **เหมือน** for examples of

common phrases with **กัน**.

ทั้งสามประเทศจะได้ปรึกษาหารือกัน

All three countries will consult (each other).

c.f. ทั้งสามประเทศจะได้ปรึกษาหารือ<u>กับ</u>สหประชาชาติ

The three countries will consult with the United Nations.

เราได้รู้จักกันโดยบังเอิญ

We got to know each other by chance.

เข้าใจกันว่าการทดลองจะมีขึ้นในระยะสองสามสัปดาห์นี้

It is understood that the experiment will take place in two to three weeks.

เขาต่างเกลียดชังกัน

They hate each other.

การสนทนากัน

The discussion

กับ

A preposition used:

> a) to express accompaniment; *with, and*

เขาพูดโทรศัพท์กับประธานาธิบดี

He spoke by phone with the president.

> b) to link nouns; *and*

การกระทบกระทั่งกันระหว่างประเทศกัมพูชากับ

ลาว

The friction between Cambodia and Laos

เมืองกับท่าเรือสมุทรปราการ

The city and harbour of Samut Prakan.

การ

A noun meaning *activity, matter, affair.* It is used:

a) in its primary sense

ไม่มีใครรู้เรื่องงานนี้ดีนอกจากคุณ

There is no one apart from you who can do this work.

การต่างประเทศ

Foreign Affairs

b) to derive nouns from action verbs. Much more common in writing than speech.

ปกครอง - การปกครอง

to govern - governance

การเป็นผู้รู้จักรับความคิดเห็นของผู้อื่น

receptivity (the state of being a person who knows how to accept the opinion of others.)

c) to derive nouns from other nouns

เมือง - การเมือง

country/city - politics

วิธี - วิธีการ
BOTH mean method/technique

การที่

This phrase nominalizes a phrase. It can often be translated as: *the fact that*.

การที่นายกรัฐมนตรีเลิกการเจรจากับพรรด ประชาธิปัตย์

The fact that the Prime Minister broke off discussions with the Democrats...

การที่เขาได้ตำแหน่งสูงนี้เพราะเขารู้จักคนใหญ่คนโต ในกรุง

He has attained this position because he knows important people in the capital.

กำลัง

A noun, literally meaning *energy* or *power*, which is used to indicate the progressive aspect of a verb in either the present or the past. It can be strengthened by placing อยู่ at the end of the phrase. Combined with จะ can have two meanings: 1) to be about to 2) no change in meaning.

เขากำลังคิดอะไรนั้นไม่มีผู้ใดทราบ

Nobody knew what he was thinking.

สหรัฐกำลังหารือกับพันธมิตร

The USA was/is consulting with her allies.

ในตอนนั้นเขากำลังจะเรียนวิทยาศาสตร์

At that time he was studying science.

กรมตำรวจกำลังจะร่างประกาศ

The police department is drafting an order...

 กี่

A quantifier meaning:

a) *how many?*

รู้ไหมว่าประเทศไทยแบ่งออกเป็นกี่จังหวัด

Do you know how many provinces there are in Thailand? (Lit:
Do you know that Thailand is divided up into how many
provinces?)

It is also used in the following expressions:

a) **ไม่กี่** - *a few, several.*

ก่อนหน้านี้ไม่กี่วันประเทศอังกฤษได้เดินทัพเข้า

ประเทศพม่า

A few days before, Britain had invaded Myanmar.

b) **กี่** classifier **ก็ได้** - *as many ... as desired, any amount at   all.*

คุณจะเอาเพื่อนไปกี่คนก็ได้

You can take as many friends as you like.

c) **เมื่อกี้นี้** - *just now.*

เธอมาถึงเมื่อกี้นี้

She's just arrived.

เกิน

A verb meaning *to exceed, be excessive*. It is used:

a) in its primary sense

ราคาจะต้องไม่เกิน 10 บาท

The price must not exceed 10 Baht.

คุณได้ทำเกินกว่าพอเสียอีก

You have done more than enough.

b) to express the meaning *too (much)*. In this sense it is often followed by **ไป**

เขาทำงานหนักเกินไป

He works too hard.

ดอกเบี้ยแพงเกินไป

The interest rate is too expensive.

เกี่ยว

A verb meaning *to be related to, connected with*. It is often followed by **กัน** and is used in the following ways:

a) in its primary sense, both alone and with the preposition **ข้อง**

นี่ไม่เกี่ยวกับผม/เรื่องนี้ไม่เกี่ยวกับผม

This does not concern me.

เขาเกี่ยวข้องกับเรื่องนี้

He is connected with this affair.

b) as the equivalent of *about,* in the sense of *in connection with, regarding.*

ข่าวเล่าลือเกี่ยวกับการหลบหนีของหน้าเหลี่ยม

Rumours relating to the flight of "Square Face" (Thaksin Shinawatra).

เราได้รับรายงานเกี่ยวกับการกระทำของเขา

We have received a report about his activities.

เกือบ

An adverb meaning *almost*. Used in a similar way to English, occasionally followed by จะ

เขาเกือบจะหายดีแล้ว

He is almost well.

พ่อเกือบมีเวลาไม่พอที่จะกินอาหาร

Dad almost didn't have time to eat.

บ้านของผมสร้างเกือบจะเสร็จแล้ว

My house is almost completed.

ในเกือบทุกประการ

In almost every way

แก่

A preposition denoting direction or motion towards a person or object. It is translated as *to* or less frequently *for* or *against*.

เขามอบจดหมายไว้แก่ผม

He committed the letter to my care.

การให้ประกันแก่ประชากร

The granting of guarantees to the people...

เครื่องมือที่เราใช้แก่ผู้เป็นศัตรของรัฐ

The weapons we use against those who are enemies of the state...

ประโยชน์แก่มนุษย์ชาติทั้งปวง

A benefit for all mankind.

ขณะ

A noun meaning *time*. It is used

    a) in its literal sense:

ขณะนั้นเองประตูก็เปิดออก

At that very instant the door opened.

ขณะนี้

Now/ at present (literally: this time)

    b) as a conjunction in the sense of *as* or *while*. In this usage it may may followed by ที่

ขณะผมเดินออกจากวัดพระแก้วความประทับใจ
อันแรกของผมคือ

As I walked out of Wat Phra Kaew my first impression was...

ขณะที่ผมเดินไปตามถนน

As I was walking along the street...

ขอ

A verb meaning *to ask, request*. Used:

a) as a main verb in its literal sense:

เขามาที่โรงเรียนเราเพื่อขอความช่วยเหลือ

He came to our school to ask for assistance.

b) to denote a desire, somewhat softer than the more abrupt

เอา

ขอน้ำชาเพิ่มหน่อยครับ

I would like a little more tea.

c) to express the polite imperative

ขอให้ผมเป็นผู้รับผิดเพียงคนเดียวเถิดครับ

Please permit me to be the sole person responsible.

ขอให้ฉันพูดเถอะ

Please let me speak.

ข้อ

A noun meaning *topic, item* It is also used:

a) as a formative element in a noun phrase.

ตกลง - ข้อตกลง

agree - agreement

ยกเว้น - ข้อยกเว้น

to except/cancel - exception

หารือ - ข้อหารือ

to consult – consultation

b) as a classifier

คำถามข้อนี้

This question

ของ

A noun meaning *thing* or *possession* which is used:

a) in its primary sense

เอาของเหล่านั้นไปเสียจากโต๊ะ

Take those things off the table.

b) as a link between two nouns in a possessive relationship. The word order is the inverse of the English and so it could be thought of as meaning "of".

บ้านที่คุณอยู่เป็นของเรา

The house you are staying in is ours.

โฆษกของกระทรวงการต่างประเทศ

The spokesman of the Ministry of Foreign Affairs

ภัยของลัทธิชาตินิยม

The danger of nationalism

ข้าง

A noun meaning *side*. It is used as the first element in a series of compounds in the formation of adverbs of time and place.

เขาคอยอยู่ข้างล่าง

He is waiting below.

เชิญเข้าข้างใน

Please come in.

เขามองขึ้นไปข้างบน

He looked up(wards).

ผมได้ยินเสียงข้างหน้า

I heard a voice ahead.

ภายใน 2-3 เดือนข้างหน้า

In the next two to three months...

ขึ้น

A verb meaning *to go up, ascend*. Used:

    a) in its primary sense:

ดาวนี้ขึ้นเวลาเย็น

This star rises in the evening.

b) as a secondary verb denoting movement upwards in either a literal or figurative sense. In this usage it   can be thought of "up" in the second part of an English phrasal verb.

ผมหยิบจดหมายนั้นขึ้นมาอ่านต่อไป

I picked up the letter and continued to read.

ผมลุกขึ้นน

I stood up.

กองทัพอากาศได้สร้างสนามบินขึ้นในจังหวัดเชียงราย

The Air Force have constructed (built up) an airport in Chiang Rai province.

c) as the second element in a comparative phrase which indicates an increase or improvement.

ดีขึ้น

Better

ราคาแพงขึ้นน

The prices are more expensive.

เขา

The most common 3rd person pronoun. It is used for both singular and plural (although the plural can be explicitly marked by the addition of

พวก meaning group). It is NOT used for animals or things. There are also some idiomatic usages, see the last example

เขาและผมได้ทำงานร่วมกัน

She/he and I have worked together.

เพื่อนของเขา

His/her friend

เขาเหล่านี้

These individuals

เข้า

A verb meaning *to enter.* Used:

a) in its primary sense.

เขาเปิดประตูแล้วเข้ามา

He opened the door and went in.

b) as a secondary verb indicating motion inwards.

เปิดประตูเดี๋ยวนี้มิฉะนั้นฉันจะยิงเข้าไป

Open the door now or I'll shoot (lit. fire in).

คง (จะ)

An auxiliary adverb which precedes the main verb. It has a range of meaning which seem contradictory to foreign, and particularly Western, learners ranging from *certainly, surely* (when it often does not need to be translated) all the way to *may be* or *perhaps*.

ความจำของคุณคงจะดีขึ้นกว่านี้อีกมาก

(Surely) your memory is much better than this.

ผมหวังใจว่าการไปเที่ยวครั้งนี้คงได้ประโยชน์มาก

I hope your trip has been beneficial.

คงจะ

Perhaps.

คน

A noun meaning *person*. It is also used:

a) as a neutral classifier for people

ลูกสามคน

three children

b) as a formative element in constructing agentive nouns from nouns and verbs

งาน - คนงาน

work – a worker

กลาง - คนกลาง

middle – mediator

ใช้ - คนใช้

use – a servant

c) some frequent idiomatic uses

คนเดียว

alone

คนทั่วไป

people (in general)

ครั้ง

A classifier meaning *time, occasion.*

ทุกครั้งที่เปิดประตูผมคิดว่า

Every time the door opened I thought...

ผมได้พบท่านประธานาธิบดีเพียงสี่ ห้าครั้ง

I only met the president four or five times.

ก่อนสงครามครั้งนี้

Before the current war...

คราว

A classifier meaning *time, turn.* The general word for time is **เวลา**

คราวหนึ่งผู้อำนวยการสั่งให้เขาออกจากห้อง

Once the director ordered him to leave the room.

ถึงคราวของคุณบ้างแล้ว

Your turn has come.

คราวหน้า

The next time...

ครึ่ง

A number-word meaning *half*. Note the word order in the second example.

ครึ่งวัน

half a day

หนึ่งวันครึ่ง

one and a half days

เวลาได้ล่วงเลยไปครึ่งชั่วโมง

Half an hour passed.

ผู้ประท้วงมากกว่าครึ่งถูกจับไปแล้ว

More than half the protesters have been arrested.

ควร (จะ)

A model verb denoting obligation, translated as *ought* or *should*.

เราควรมีการเลือกตั้งที่เป็นเสรี

We should have free elections

ผมควรจะถูกตำหนิอย่างนี้ละหรือ

Should I be criticised in this way?

ผมคิดว่าคุณควรกินอาหารเสียบ้าง

I think you should eat some food.

เราควรไปเรียกคนอืนๆมา

We ought to go and ask some other people to come.

ความ

Used to derive abstract nouns from verbs of state, i.e. verbs which correspond to adjectives in English. The distinction between **ความ** and **การ** is blurred and the student should make a note of words which seem to take the "wrong" prefix. Unlike **การ**, **ความ** is equally common in speech and writing.

ดี - ความดี

good – goodness

ร่วมมือ - ความร่วมมือ

to co-operate – co-operation

คิด - ความคิด

to think – idea

ตกลง - ความตกลงกัน

to agree - agreement

ไม่มีความสงสัยในตนเอง

self-confidence (lit. the state of not having doubts about oneself.)

ค่อย

An adverb which is used:

a) in its positive form to mean *gradually* (often doubled)

ถนนค่อยๆโค้งไปทางทิศใต้

The road gradually curves to the south.

สภาพคนไข้ค่อยดีขึ้น

The patient's condition is gradually improving.

b) with the negative marker ไม่, it means *not likely, hardly, scarcely.*

ผมไม่ค่อยเชื่อเสียแล้ว

I can hardly believe it.

ลาวไม่ค่อยเต็มใจจะรับความช่วยเหลือจาก ประเทศไทย

Laos is not likely to accept aid from Thailand.

คำ

A noun meaning *word.* Used to derive nouns from some verbs.

ตอบ - คำตอบ

to reply – a reply

สั่ง - คำสั่ง

to order – an order

สัญญา - คำสัญญา

to promise – a promise

สอน - คำสอน

to teach – teaching, doctrine

คือ

A verb which is used as a copula – that is when the verb *to be* links two phrases which are identical. To link a noun to a descriptive phrase you should use **เป็น** or nothing.

ราชอาณาจักรไทย คือเมืองไทย
The Kingdom of Thailand, that is to say Thailand

ประเทศที่เขากำลังพูดถึงอยู่นี้ก็คือสหรัฐอเมริกา
The country he is referring to is the USA.

นี่คือการตัดสินใจของคุณหรือ
Is this your decision?

เคย

An adverb meaning *ever.* Used:

a) to impart an imperfective aspect to a past phrase.

ชวรัตน์เคยเป็นมือขวาของสมชาย
Chaovarat was once Somchai's right-hand man.

b) in the negative, *never.*

เขาไม่เคยพูดถึงเรื่องอื่นๆเลย
He never talks about anything else.

ผมไม่เคยไปเที่ยวภาคอีสาน (ไปเที่ยว is used for

visiting place; **ไปเยี่ยม** is used for visiting people)
I've never visited Isaan.

c) *ever,* in a question.

คุณเคยได้ยินเรื่องเช่นนี้บ้างไหม

Have you ever heard a story like this?

d) in certain set phrases.

เช่นเคย

as usual

เครื่อง

A noun meaning *machine, implement*. It is used:

a) to create impersonal agent nouns, most frequently from verbs:

บิน - เครื่องบิน

to fly – aeroplane

แต่งตัว - เครื่องแต่งตัว

to dress – clothing

มือ - เครื่องมือ

hand – instrument

b) as a classifier for some machines and appliances.

เขายกหูโทรศัพท์เครื่องหนึ่งในจำนวนหลายเครื่องที่ตั้งอยู่บนโต๊ะ

He picked up the receiver of one of the many phones which

were on the table.

ใคร

a) The interrogative pronoun *who*.

ใครกล่าวเช่นนั้น

Who said so?

b) The indefinite pronoun *anyone, anybody*.

มีใครอีก

Is there anybody else?

ไม่มีใครที่พูดคำเมืองได้เลย

There isn't anyone who speaks Northern Thai..

c) when it's doubled, it means *everyone*.

ใครๆชอบเขาทั้งนั้น

Everyone likes him.

จง

A pre-verb auxiliary used to introduce an imperative. It may be used with **อย่า** to express a negative imperative also.

จงทำเท่าที่คุณทำได้

Do as much as you can.

จงมาหาเรา

Do come and see us.

จงอย่าวางใจพวกที่แสร้งทำตัวเป็นมิตรกับรัฐบาลเรา
เลย

Don't trust those who pretend to be friends of our government.

จน

Means *until* - beware that this covers both the conjunction and preposition although a distinction can be made in Thai. See the examples below:

a) as a conjunction it is often followed by **กว่า** or **กระทั่ง**.

นั่งลงก่อนจนกว่าจะถูกเรียกตัว

b) as a preposition, meaning *until* or *up to*.

ผมจับความหมายไม่ได้จนกระทั่งต่อมาอีกนาน

I didn't get he meaning until a long time afterwards.

เรานั่งพูดกันจนรุ่งสาง

We sat chatting until dawn.

จะ

An auxiliary verb with a range of uses – primarily covering the future or uncertainty.

a) To express the future – the equivalent of *will*.

ราคาจะสูงขึ้น

Prices will go up.

b) To express the conditional form of the verb in reported speech when the verb in the main is in the past tense. The use   of the conditional is a quirk of English idiom, Thai is more logical in preserving the tense of the original statement.

นายกรัฐมนตรีได้ยืนยันว่าจะไม่เปลี่ยนท่าที

The Prime Minister declared emphatically that he would not change his position. (His actual words were: I will not change my position.)

เราได้นัดที่จะพบกันอีก

We agreed to meet again.

c) To link may pre-verbal auxiliaries and modal verbs to the

main verb. In this use the จะ is optional and it is extremely difficult for the foreign learner to use idiomatically, although incorrect use will seldom impede comprehension.

ไม่มีข่าวที่จะแจ้งให้

There is no news to give (you).

ญี่ปุ่นปรารถนาจะได้รับ 20 000 กิโล

Japan wishes to obtain 20,000 kilos.

จาก

A verb meaning *to leave, depart*. It is used:

a) in its primary sense.

เขาจากเมื่อสิบนาทีมาแล้ว

He left ten minutes ago.

b) as a preposition meaning *of, from, by means of*.

รถยนต์ที่สั่งซื้อจากต่างประเทศ

The cars which were ordered from abroad.

พวกผู้ลับลอบได้ถูกปราบปรามจากรัฐบาล

The smugglers have been suppressed by the government.

จึง

A pre-verbal adverb (i.e. it comes before the verb – see examples below) which indicates that the second clause is a consequence of the action in the first clause. It can be translated as *so* or *then*, although it can be left untranslated.

ไม่มีใครตอบเขาจึงพูดอีกว่า

Nobody answered so he said again...

ชาวเรือจับปลาพากันตกใจจึงรีบแจวเข้าฝั่ง

The crew of the fishing boat were frightened so they rowed quickly to the shore.

ผมทนอยู่ไม่ได้จึงถามขึ้นว่า

I couldn't stand it any longer so I asked...

จากเหตุข้อนี้เขาจึงไปเสีย

Because of this he went away.

ฉะนั้น

A conjunction meaning *therefore* or *so.* Its negative form is มิฉะนั้น, which means *or else, otherwise.* It is a bookish phrase with ก็ and จึง much more common in speech.

เขาต้องการหนังสือเล่มนี้ฉะนั้นฉันจึงให้

He wanted this book so I gave it to him.

เช่น

A noun meaning *manner* or pattern. It is used in a similar way to prepositions as *like, as* or *such as*. This construction is very common in Thai but for the beginner trying to translate into Thai it can be a very useful way of expressing complex ideas. **อย่าง** covers similar ground but is normally used to form adverb from adjectives.

ความเคลื่อนไหวเช่นนี้

Movements like this...

สถานการณ์เช่นนี้

A situation such as this...

ถ้าเช่นนั้น

In that case...

ผมไม่ใช่คนเดียวที่มีความรู้สึกเช่นนี้

I am not the only person who feels like this.

ใช่

An adjective meaning *to be correct, be so*. It is also used:

a) in conjunction with **ไหม** to form a tag question.

ร้อนมากกว่าที่อังกฤษ ใช่ไหม

It's a lot hotter than England, isn't it?

b) in conjunction with **ไม่** to form the negative forms of **คือ** and **เป็น**.

เขาไม่ใช่นักการเมือง

He isn't a politician

เป็นหน้าที่ของเราทุกคนต้องช่วยรัฐบาลไม่ใช่ตำหนิรัฐบาล

It is the duty of everyone to support the government, not to criticise it.

ซึ่ง

A relative pronoun. Very much restricted to the written language.

นายกรัฐมนตรีซึ่งกำลังอยู่ที่ภาคใต้

The prime minister, who is currently in the South,...

เขามีผู้ช่วยสองคนซึ่งคนหนึ่งเป็นนายตำรวจ

He has two assistants, one of whom is a police officer.

ณ

A preposition covering any basic temporal or spatial relationship, most often *on, in* or *at*. It is an extremely formal word common in titles or set phrases. It is also used with places to form aristocratic surnames like *de* in French or *von* in German.

การ ประชุม ณ ภูเก็ต

The meeting in Phuket

เรื่องนี้เกิดขึ้น ณ เวลาเช้าวันที่สาม กุมภาพันธ์

This incident occurred on the morning of the 3rd of February.

ณ สงขลา

Na-Songkhla – a surname.

ด้วย

A multi-functional word generally connoting togetherness. Used:

a) as a preposition denoting means, accompaniment or purposed. Translated as *by, with* or *for*. It is frequently used with abstract nouns with **ความ** to form adverbial phrases.

รถแล่นไปด้วยไฟฟ้า

The car runs on electricity.

เขาต่อสู้ด้วยความกล้าหาญ

He fought with courage.

b) an adverb meaning *too, also.*

ผมจะไปด้วย

I'll go too.

c) in the phrase **ด้วยกัน** meaning *together.*

เราอยู่กินด้วยกัน

We live together (as a couple).

ดัง

A preposition meaning *according to, like.* It is now largely restricted to set phrases.

ดังกล่าว
The aforementioned...

ดังนั้น
Like that; thus...

เหตุผลมีดังต่อไปนี้
The reasons are as follows.

เราจะจัดส่งผู้เชี่ยวชาญดังกล่าวเดินทางยัง

ประเทศไทย
We shall arrange to send these (lit. the aforementioned) experts to Thailand.

เดิม

An adjective meaning *former, previous*. Its translation will vary considerably depending on context.

เขายึดความเห็นเดิม
He held his original opinion.

เดียว

An adjective meaning *only, single, alone*. When used with **กับ** or **กัน**, it means *(the) same*.

คำเดียว
A single word...

เขาทำคนเดียวก็ได้

He can do it alone.

ในสัปดาห์เดียวกัน

In the same week

โดย

A preposition meaning *by, with* or *from*. It is often used to transform entire phrases into adverbial expressions.

หาทางตกลงกันโดยสันติวิธี

to seek an agreement through peaceful means.

โดยเหตุนี้

For this reasons.

การวางตัวบุคคลเป็นไปโดยไม่ถูกต้อง

The assignment of personnel was not carried out correctly.

เขาล้มต้นไม้โดยใช้ขวาน

He felled the tree with an axe.

เขาทำงานโดยไม่มีระเบียบ

He works without a system.

ใด

An indefinite or interrogative adjective, meaning *any, whatever, which?*

ไม่มีความจำเป็นประการใดที่จะทำเช่นนั้น

There isn't any necessity for doing so.

ชาติเป็นกลางไม่ว่าชาติใด

Any neutral nation...

ผู้ใดสนใจจะมาตรวจดูได้

Anybody who is interested can come and inspect it.

ไม่ว่ากรณีใดๆ

For whatever reason...

ได้

A wide range of largely unconnected meanings.

a) as a primary verb meaning *to get, obtain*.

ทุนรอนที่ได้จากประเทศจีน

The capital which was obtained from China...

b) as an auxiliary to mark the past tense. This is quite difficult for foreigners to use actively, it is best to listen and copy   native examples.

กองทัพอากาศได้รับคำสั่งจากกรุงเทพฯ

The Air Force received an order from Bangkok.

c) a sentence final particle meaning *to be able, can*. The   English translation covers two concepts, for a learnt skill   (such as swimming or speaking a language) **เป็น** should be   used.

หากไทยและกัมพูชาไม่อาจจะตกลงกันได้

If Thailand and Cambodia cannot agree.

d) as an auxiliary expressing the idea *to get to, to have the chance to*. In this sense it is often untranslated.

คณะกรรมการจะได้พิจารณาเรื่องนี้

The committee will investigate this matter.

e) in certain set phrases with ก็

เมื่อไรก็ได้

any time, any time will do

ใครก็ได้

anybody (at all)

ตน

The reflexive pronoun *self*. It is frequently combined by เอง.

พรุ่งนี้ผมจะไปรายงานที่กรมด้วยตนเอง

Tomorrow I will go and report to the department tomorrow.

เขาได้กลับสู่บ้านเมืองของตนเอง

He returned to his own country.

ทุกคนทำงานเพื่อตนเอง

Everyone works for himself.

ตลอด

An adjective meaning *throughout, entirely*. It is often used with ทั้ง

and ทั้งหมด

เขานอนหลับตลอดทั้งวัน

He sleeps all day.

ไม่มีใครสักคนเดียวตลอดทั้งถนน

There isn't anyone along the whole road.

นายพลผู้นี้บังบัญชากองทัพตลอดทั้งหมด

The General has the entire command of the army.

ข้าวนั้นปลูกกันตลอดทั่วประเทศไทย

Rice is grown all over Thailand.

ต่อ

A preposition denoting direction towards an object in both a literal and figurative sense. Its translation depends on the English idiom, variously *to, for, in* or *against*.

เขาต้องรายงานเรื่องนี้ต่อตำรวจ

He must report this matter to the police.

ข่าวใหญ่ที่มีความสำคัญต่อโลกทั้งโลก

Very important news for the whole world...

ต่อ

A verb meaning *to continue*. Used:

    a) in its primary sense.

ถนนสายนี้จะต่อไปถึงหัวหิน

This road continues to Hua Hin

b) in conjunction with **มา** or **ไป** to form adverbial phrases of time.

สามชั่วโมงต่อมาผมก็ได้พบเขา

I met him three hours later.

โฆษกกล่าวต่อไปว่า

The spokesman said in addition to that...

ต่อจากนั้นมา

Thereafter...

ต้อง

A modal verb which covers a range of meanings from desire to compulsion and most shades in between. It can be translated as *want, must, have to*. It is often followed by **การ** in the sense of *must.* In all

meaning it may be followed by **จะ**.

ผมจะต้องเดินทางออกจากเมือง

I will have to leave town.

เรื่องนี้ต้องพูดกันมาก

This matter requires a lot of discussion.

ตอน

A noun meaning *part, section, region*. It forms compounds which are used:

a) in spacial relationships.

ตอนกลาง

Central Thailand

b) in temporal relationships.

ในตอนนั้นเขากำลังเรียนวิชาเกษตร

At that time he was studying agriculture.

ตอนดึกคืนวันนั้นผมกลับไปบ้าน

Late that night I returned home.

ตั้ง

A verb meaning *to place, set* or *put*. It is used:

a) in its primary sense.

เราจะตั้งค่าย

We will set up camp.

b) in a temporal expressions with the meaning *from* or for. In this sense it is often followed by แต่.

ตั้งแต่เช้าจนตกดึก

From morning till late at night...

ผมอยู่ที่นี่มาตั้งเจ็ดปีแล้ว

I have been here for seven years.

ตัว

A reflexive pronoun. Used:

a) in its primary sense.

ผู้ชายมักเห็นแก่ตัว

Men are selfish (lit. they look to themselves.)

ผมได้เตรียมตัวไว้สำหรับตอนนี้แล้ว

I have already prepared myself for this.

b) as a classifier for animals (but NOT elephants) and some other nouns.

ม้าสองตัว

Two horses...

ต่าง

An adjective meaning *to be different, various*. It is used:

a) in its primary sense (often reduplicated).

เขาลาออกด้วยเหตุประการต่างๆ

He resigned for various reasons.

แต่ในส่วนเขานั้นต่างกันมาก

But with him it's quite different.

b) to emphasise the plurality of a preceding noun.

ทุกคนต่างตื่นเต้น

Everyone become excited.

c) idiomatically with **ประเทศ** to mean *abroad, foreign.*

กระทรวงการต่างประเทศ

The ministry of foreign affairs.

ตาม

A verb meaning *to follow.* It is used:

a) in its primary sense.

เขาสั่งให้ผมตามไป

He ordered me to follow.

b) with a following **ที่** to mean *as, just as*.

ตามที่ได้กล่าวมาแล้ว

As has already been stated...

c) as preposition meaning *in conformity with, according to.*

ตามข่าวจากกระทรวงมหาดไทย

According to reports from the ministry of the interior.

ตามทัณฑวิธีถูกต้อง

In conformity with the correct methods...

d) as a preposition meaning *along.*

เมืองต่างๆตามชายฝั่งทะเล

Various cities along the coast...

e) In certain idiomatic phrases.

ตามความจริง

In truth, actually...

อย่างไรก็ตาม

In any event, nevertheless...

แต่

A range of unconnected meanings.

a) A conjunction, *but*.

ผมจะพยายามแต่คงไม่ได้ง่ายนัก

I'll try but it won't be easy.

b) as an adverb meaning *only*.

นี่เป็นแค่เพียงคำแนะนำ

This is only a word of advice.

เขาไม่แต่จะเสียชื่อเท่านั้นยังต้องฉิบหายด้วย

They are not only discredited but also ruined.

c) as a temporal preposition meaning *from*.

กฎหมายนี้มีผลบังคับตั้งแต่วันที่สามเดือนนี้

The law goes into effect as of the third of this month.

d) In combination with **ละ** to mean *each*. Note the word order.

สมาชิกแต่ละคน

Each member...

ถ้า

A conjunction corresponding to *if*, and occasionally *when*. It is sometimes followed by **หาก** to reinforce its meaning.

ถ้ามีเหตุการณ์ฉุกเฉิน
If there is an emergency

คุณไปก็ได้ถ้าอยากไป
You can go if you like.

ถ้าหากว่ารัฐบาลได้ระดมกำลังทุ่มเท
If the government exerts all its efforts...

ถึง

A verb meaning *to arrive, reach*. Used:

    a) in its primary sense.

คุณพ่อถึงบ้านก่อนฉัน
Dad got home before me.

    b) as a secondary verb to act as preposition meaning *to, about, concerning*.

นายทหารเวียดนาม 5 คนได้เดินทางมาถึงเมืองฮานอย
Five Vietnamese officers travelled to Hanoi.

ผมไม่พูดถึงการเมืองเลย

I didn't speak about politics at all.

ถูก

A verb meaning *to suffer*. It is used to form the equivalent of the passive tense. It should be noted that the passive is less frequent in Thai, even in formal registers. This word should not be confused with

its homonym **ถูก** meaning *to be cheap*.

เขาถูกตำรวจจับ

He was arrested by the police.

ถูกยิงตายไปอีกคนหนึ่งแล้ว

Another person was shot to death.

ทรง

A prefix which is added to verbs when the subject is a king or god.

กษัตริย์แห่งกัมพูชาทรงต้อนรับคณะบุคคลสำคัญของ ฝรั่งเศส

The king of Cambodia received a group of important Frenchman.

ทั้ง

An adjective denoting wholeness or completeness. It is used:

a) as the word for *all, whole*.

คนทั้งนั้น

All these people...

b) with **สอง** to mean *both*

ผู้เขียนทั้งสองคน

Both writers...

c) in the compounds **รวมทั้ง** (*including*) and **ทั้งหมด** (*all together, wholly*)

คนตายเจ็ดคนรวมทั้งรัฐมนตรี

Seven people died including the minister.

เขามิได้เลวไปทั้งหมด

He's not all bad.

ทั้งหมดราคาเท่าไร

How much does it cost altogether?

ทั่ว

An adjective meaning *to be general, universal*. It is also used

a) as a preposition meaning *all over*.

ข้าวนั้นปลูกกันตลอดทั่วประเทศไทย

Rice is grown all over Thailand.

b) when followed by **ไป** as an adverb meaning *generally, universally*.

เขาได้รับความชมเชยทั่วไป

He was universally admired.

กล่าวโดยทั่วไป

Generally speaking...

ทาง

A noun meaning *road, way* and more abstractly *method*. It is used:

a) in its primary sense.

เชิญทางนี้ครับ

This way, please!

เขาไม่มีทางจะทราบข้อความอื่นใดนอกเหนือ ไปจากที่ทางเจ้าหน้าที่ประสงค์ให้ได้ทราบ

They had no way of knowing anything other than that which   the officials wanted them to know.

b) as a preposition meaning *by* or *via*.

การลำเลียงยุทธสัมภาระทางอากาศ

The shipment of military supplies by air.

เขามาทางลำปาง

He came via Lampang.

c) to link nouns together in cases when English would use an adjective and noun.

การประชุมทางการเมือง

A political conference...

d) to mark the subject of the sentence.

ทางเจ้าหน้าที่ฝ่ายเราก็มิได้ยิงโต้ตอบ

Our officers did not return fire.

e) in the compound **ทางการ** meaning *official* or *officials*.

ไม่มีเอกสารเป็นทางการเลย

There are no official documents.

ท่าน

An honorific word used:

a) as a second person pronoun.

ท่านกำลังจะมีความจำเป็นสำหรับผม

I am going to need you.

b) as a third person pronoun.

ท่านได้ให้สัมภาษณ์

He gave an interview.

c) a classifier for high ranking persons.

ผู้มีเกียรติหลายท่าน

Several famous people...

d) a prefix placed before titles.

ท่านประธานาธิบดีจะแจ้งให้รัฐสภาทราบ

The president will inform the congress...

ทำไม

An interrogative pronoun meaning *why*. When it appears at the end of the phrase it is often followed by **ละ**

ทำไมคุณไม่พูดอะไรบ้างล่ะ

Why don't you say anything?

หัวเราะทำไมละ

Why are you laughing?

ที

A noun meaning *time* or *occasion*. Used in several compounds which function as adverbs of time. Note also the idiomatic phrase meaning *very, quite, extremely.*

ทีแรกเขาทำเป็นไม่เข้าใจ

At first he pretended not to understand.

พรุ่งนี้มาอีกที

Come again tomorrow.

ผมลุกขึ้นทันที

I got up immediately.

ถูกทีเดียว

That's quite right.

ที่

A relative pronoun covering *which, who* and *that*. It is used:

a) in its primary sense.

วันที่สงครามอุบัติขึ้น

The day the war started...

กลุ่มประเทศที่นับถือศาสนาพุทธ

The bloc of countries which adheres to Buddhism...

b) as a link between a noun and a following verb, often translated into English with an infinitive or gerund (-ing).

ความพยายามที่จะใช้อิทธิพล

An effort to use influence...

ความคิดที่จะให้จีนเป็นชาติพัฒนาแล้ว

The idea of considering China a developed country...

ที่

A noun meaning *place*. It is used:

a) in its primary sense.

ที่นอกเมืองหลายแห่ง

Several places outside of the city...

b) as a preposition meaning *in* or *at*.

โรงงานผลิตเครื่องบินที่เมืองกรุงเทพฯ

The aeroplane factory in the city of Bangkok

เขาอยู่ที่ประตู

He is at the door.

เรามีการประชุมกันที่ที่ทำงาน

We held a meeting at our place of work.

ที่

A formative element used to derive ordinal (1st, 2nd, etc) from cardinal numbers (1,2, etc)

สงครามโลกครั้งที่สอง

Second World War

ในวันที่สามธันวาคม

On the third of December

ทุก

An adjective meaning *each* or *every*. It can be reduplicated to intensify its meaning, although sometimes this is just idiomatic.

เขามาทุกๆวัน

He comes every day.

เราทำทุกสิ่งทุกอย่างทันทีไม่ได้

We can't do everything at once.

เท่า

An adjective meaning *to be equal*. It is used:

a) in its primary sense.

มนุษย์ทุกคนเท่ากัน

All men are equal

b) with **กับ** to form the comparative of equality (*as...as*)

เขารู้เท่ากับเรา

He knows as much as us.

คุณรู้ดีเท่ากับฉันว่า

You know as well as I do that...

c) as a component of the compounds **เท่าไร** (*how much?*)

and **เท่านั้น** (*only, that's all*).

มีคนเท่าไร

How many people are there?

มีเสียงคัดค้านสองสามคนเท่านั้น

Only two or three people voiced their opinion.

แทน

A verb originally meaning *to replace, substitute*. It is most often used in the sense of *instead (of)*. When it precedes a verb it is followed by **ที่จะ**.

แทนที่จะกลับไปพนมเปญ

Instead of returning to Phnom Penh...

คุณต้องไปแทนผม

You must go instead of me.

ผู้แทน
Representative (one who substitutes).

แทบ

An adverb meaning *almost*. When it qualifies a verb it may be
followed by จะ

แทบจะกล่าวได้
One can almost say...

เราเหนื่อยแทบทุกคน
Almost all of us were tired.

แทบไม่มีที่จะยืน
There was almost nowhere to stand.

นอก

A preposition with primary meaning *outside (of)*. It is also used with
จาก to mean *except, besides*.

ที่นอกเมืองหลายแห่ง
Several places outside of the city.

เมืองนอก
Foreign countries...

นอกจากว่าเขาพูดเร็วเกินไปแล้วนับว่าเขาเป็นคนสอนดีมาก

Except for the fact that he speaks too fast, he is an excellent teacher.

นอกจากนี้

Besides this...

นัก

A formative element used to derive trades from other words, both nouns and verbs.

หนังสือพิมพ์ - นักหนังสือพิมพ์

Newspaper - journalist

ประวัติศาสตร์ - นักประวัติศาสตร์

History – historian

บิน - นักบิน

to fly – pilot

เขียน - นักเขียน

to write – writer

นั่น นั้น

These two both mean *that, those*. The first is the **pronoun** (used on its own) and the latter is the **adjective** (used after the noun phrase). It occasionally corresponds to the English definite article, *the*.

นั่นคือพ่อ

That is my father.

นั่นไม่สำคัญ

That isn't important.

ที่นั่น

There...

ในฤดูร้อนปีนั้น

In the summer of that year...

วันที่ผมมาหาคุณนั้น

That day that I came to see you...

น่า

A formative element which is prefixed to verbs to produce adjectives meaning *to be worth....* The English translation will vary from case to case.

สนใจ - น่าสนใจ

to interest – interesting

เข้าใจ - น่าเข้าใจ

to understand – understandable

อ่าน - น่าอ่าน

to read - legible

รัก - น่ารัก

to love - lovable

นาน

An adverb meaning *to be long (time)*. Used mostly as a secondary verb with the meaning *for a long time*.

ผมอยากจะพูดกับคุณนานมาแล้ว

I have wanted to talk to you for a long time.

วันนี้เราจะพบกันไม่นานนัก

We won't meet for very long today.

คุณนั่งอยู่ที่นี่นานเท่าใดแล้ว

How long have you been sitting here?

นาย

A noun meaning *master*. It is also used to form agentive nouns from nouns and verbs.

ทุน - นายทุน

capital, wealth – capitalist

ตำรวจ - นายตำรวจ

police – police officer

ทหาร - นายทหาร

soldier – (military) officer

จ้าง - นายจ้าง

to hire – to employer

นี่ นี้

These two both mean *this, these*. The first is the **pronoun** (used on its own) and the latter is the **adjective** (used after the noun phrase. It occasionally corresponds to the English definite article, *the*.

นี่หรือหนังสือที่อ่าน

Are these the books you are reading?

นี่เป็นรายงานของเรา

This is our report.

มานี่

Come here!

ครูใหม่ทั้งสองคนนี้

Both these two new teachers...

โรงงานนี้มีคนงานประมาณหนึ่งพัน

This factory has about a thousand workers.

เนื่อง

An adjective often followed by จาก meaning *to be resultant from, be caused by*. It is quite bookish and is used:

a) as a conjunction, *because, since*.

เนื่องจากเราทราบดีว่าเป็นคนใกล้ชิดเขาคน หนึ่ง เราจึงก็ตั้งใจฟังคำกล่าวของเขา

Since we knew that he was very close to him, we attentively to what he said.

b) as a preposition, *out of, because of, on account of*.

เนื่องจากเหตุข้อนี้เขาจึงไปเสีย

Because of this he went away.

เขาถามเนื่องจากความอยากรู้

He asked out of curiosity.

ใน

A preposition denoting location within, used with spatial, temporal and circumstantial relationships. It is a slightly bookish word and its translation varies with context from *in, on, at* or *during*.

ในประเทศไทย

In Thailand

เขาตายในสนามรบ

He died on the field of battle.

ในหกเดือนแรกของปีใหม่นี้

In the first six months of the new year...

ในครั้งนี้

At this time..

ในยามสงคราม

During the war...

เสรีภาพในการพูด

Freedom of speech

บน

A noun originally meaning *top* used primarily as a preposition meaning *on*. There are other prepositions that can be used for *on* but this one means specifically *on a flat surface*.

บนฝาผนัง

On the wall...

บนเรือ

On board (a ship)

บาง

An adjective meaning *some*. It is ALWAYS used with a classifier.

บางครั้ง

Sometimes...

นักประวัติศาสตร์บางคน

Some historians...

คนบางคน

Some people...

บ้าง

An adverb meaning *some, any, to some extent*. It can also function as a pronoun (*some*). It can be used at the end of a question to show that the asker is expect a list or multiple answers – in which cause it does not need to be translated.

ผมมีเงินอยู่บ้าง

I have some money.

ใครมีอะไรจะแถลงบ้าง

Does anyone have anything to declare?

คุณคิดว่าอะไรจะเกิดแก่ผมบ้าง

Do you think that will happen to me?

ประจำ

An adjective meaning *to be steady, attached*, but it is very often used in the written language with a wide variety of meanings. Study the examples below and when you came across this word in your studies always adopt a very open mind when it comes to translations.

เราชุมนุมกันในที่ประชุมประจำสัปดาห์

We met for our weekly meeting.

ทางทหารประจำฉะเชิงเทรา

The officers stationed at Chachoengsao...

ผู้แทนประเทศไทยประจำสหประชาชาติ

The Thai representative to the United Nations...

ประมาณ

An adverb meaning *about* or *approximately*.

กำลังทหารอเมริกันประมาณ 5000 คน

About 5000 American troops...

ประมาณกลางเดือนมิถุนายน
About the middle of June...

เป็น

The verb *to be*. It is used:

a) in its primary sense.

เขาเป็นเพื่อนผม
He is my friend.

b) as the verb *to become*.

เขาเป็นเพื่อนผม
He became my friend.

c) in certain set phrases with the meaning *to be characterized by.*

เป็นประโยชน์
be useful

เป็นระเบียบ
be orderly

d) after the main verb to express *to be able*. This is used with learnt skills and Thais will often correct you if you use it

incorrectly in place of ได้

ผมพูดอังกฤษไม่เป็น
I can't speak English

e) as a preposition meaning *as, for.*

เขามิได้เห็นประชาชนเป็นเครื่องจักร

He didn't look upon people as machines.

ไป

A verb meaning *to go*. It is used:

a) in it primary sense.

คุณอยากไปเวียงจันทร์ไหม

Do you want to go to Vientiane?

b) as a secondary verb, often with little or no additional meaning.

ไม่อยากเสียเวลาอีกต่อไป

I didn't want to waste any more time.

อย่าวิตกไปเลย

Don't worry at all.

เขาอาจถูกจับไป

He may have been captured.

ผู้

A noun meaning *person*. It is used as a formative element in forming agentive nouns from verbs and phrases.

เขียน - ผู้เขียน

To write – writer

ช่วย - ผู้ช่วย

To help – assistant

ผู้ที่วางใจได้

A person who can be trusted.

ฝ่าย

A noun meaning *side*. It is used:

a) in its primary sense.

เพื่อทำความตกลงกับฝ่ายค้าน

In order to make an agreement with the opposition...

b) To join a noun to a verb or another noun which frequently translates into English as an adjective. In   often carries the meaning of *in the sphere of*, *in the domain of, concerned with*.

คณะกรรมการฝ่ายเมือง

The municipal committee...

นครหลวงฝ่ายบริการ

The administrative capital...

เจ้าหน้าที่ฝ่ายปกครอง

The government authorities...

พร้อม

An adjective meaning *ready*; usually in the form **พร้อมที่จะ**. It is used:

a) in its primary sense.

สหายนั่งอยู่ในรถพร้อมที่จะฟังวิทยุตำรวจ

His companion is sitting in the car ready to receive police calls.

b) in the form **พร้อมกับ** meaning *(together) with.*

ผมขับรถกลับบ้านพร้อมกับเพื่อนสามคน

I drove home with three friends.

c) in the form **พร้อมๆกัน** meaning *at the same time.*

ผมสอนหนังสือถึงสามโรงเรียนพร้อมๆกัน

I am teaching in three schools at the same time.

พระ

A noun meaning *monk*. It is used as an honorific prefix to pronouns and nouns. Its extended form **พระองค์** is used as the 3rd person pronoun for kings and gods. For more details see the **ราชาสัพท์** appendix.

พระเจ้าสีหนุโรดมได้เสด็จไปตั้งกองบัญชาการของพระองค์อยู่ที่นั่น

King Norodom Sihanouk went and set up his headquarters there.

พวก

A noun meaning *group*. It is used to pluralise pronouns and certain animate nouns. Bear in mind that any noun and many pronouns can be plural without explicit marking.

นักเรียน - พวกนักเรียน
Student - students

พวกผู้หญิง
Women

พวกชาวนา
Farmers

พอ

An adjective meaning *enough*. It is used:

a) in its primary meaning both as an adjective and adverb

คุณมีเงินพอสำหรับการเดินทางแล้วหรือ
Do you have enough money for the journey?

คุณทำงานไม่พอ
You don't work enough.

b) as a conjunction meaning *as soon as*.

พอข้าศึกปรากฎตัวขึ้นกองทหารก็พากันถอย
As soon as the enemy appeared, the troops retreated.

พอผมออกมาเขาก็หยุดทำงาน
As soon as I left he stopped work.

เพราะ

A preposition originally meaning *for, because of*. It is used in this sense but more commonly followed by ว่า to mean *because*.

เพราะเหตุนี้

For this reason...

วันนี้ไปไม่ได้เพราะว่าเพลียมาก

I can't go today because I'm too tired.

เราออกจากบ้านไม่ได้เพราะฝนตก

We could not go out because it was raining.

เพิ่ง

An auxiliary adverb denoting the immediate past, often translated as *just* with the past tense.

ผมเพิ่งมาจากสิงคโปร์

I have just arrived from Singapore.

โรงงานเพิ่งตั้งขึ้น

The factory was just recently constructed.

เพียง

A noun meaning *level* or *extent*. It is most commonly used adverbially

a) in the sense of *just, only, merely* (often in the form เพียง แต่)

เขาเพียงแต่ตั้งข้อสังเกตว่า

He merely observed that...

ที่ฉันเล่ามาแล้วนั้นเป็นเพียงการเริ่มเรื่องเท่านั้น

What I have just told you already is just the beginning of the story.

b) with the suffix **ไร**, meaning *how much, to what extent.*

สำหรับงานใหญ่ๆอย่างนี้เรื่องระเบียบเป็นของสำคัญเพียงไรคุณย่อมทราบอยู่แล้ว

You doubtlessly know already how important system is in great projects of this type.

เพื่อ

A preposition, also used as a conjunction, expressing purpose. Before a verb it is translated as *in order to*; before a noun *for.*

เพื่อปราบปราม

In order to suppress...

การเตรียมตัวเพื่อการสงคราม

Preparation for war...

ผมทำเพื่อประโยชน์ของเขา

I did it for his own good.

ภาย

A noun meaning *side, section.* Used as the first element in a series of compounds denoting spatial and temporal relationships.

ประเทศรุ่งเรืองภายใต้การปกครองเขา

the country prospered under his rule.

เราไปถึงที่นั่นภายหลังที่ได้เดินทางไปสองวัน

We arrived there after two days' journey.

ภายในประเทศ

Within the country...

มัก (จะ)

An auxiliary based on a verb meaning *to like* which indicates that the main verb is likely to happen. In Lao/Isaan it is the normal word for *to like*.

ข้าราชการมักเดินทางโดยรถไฟ

Officials usually travel by train.

ผู้ชายมักเห็นแก่ตัว

Men are selfish (i.e. men like to look after themselves)

มัน

A third person pronoun used for animals and things. When used to refer to humans it has pejorative connotations. Note the peculiar idiom of using a pronoun after a subject in the second example. This is very common in Thai.

โยนมันลงไปเสียในไฟ

Throw it into the fire.

ตำรวจมันก็จะไม่สงสัยว่า

The police won't suspect that...

มันเป็นเรื่องของท่านเอง

It is your own business.

มา

A verb meaning *to come*. It is used:

a) in its primary sense.

เขามาถึงสำนักงานของผม

He came to my office.

b) as a secondary verb indicating that an action is performed towards the speaker. Often this is more idiomatic than an important grammatical marker. It is often untranslated.

ตอบมาเร็ว

Answer quickly.

เขาได้ส่งอาหารมาให้เราหลายห่อ

He sent several packages of food to us.

c) in various idiomatic phrases dealing with time. Many of these are very common and should be learnt by heart.

เขาได้ออกจากบ้านสองวันมาแล้ว

He left home two days ago.

อีกสองสามวันต่อมามีชายคนหนึ่งมาหาผม

Two or three days later a man came to see me.

มาก

An adverb covering the meanings *much, a lot, many* and *very*. The translation is always clear from context. The phrase **โดยมาก** means *mostly, generally*.

เรื่องแบบนี้ยังมีอีกมาก

There are many other stories of this type.

ข้อความมีประโยชน์มาก

The information is very useful.

คนโดยมากคิดเช่นนั้น

Most people think so.

มิ

A variant of the negative marker **ไม่**. It can be used when the following word contains an "aj" sound (**ไอ ใอ อัย อาย**). For a foreign student, you are unlikely to need to use this as **ไม่** is always understood.

เพื่อมิให้อะไรตกอยู่ในมือพวกญี่ปุ่น

In order that nothing may fall into the hands of the Japanese...

สงครามอันมิได้ประกาศ

An undeclared war...

มี

A verb meaning *to have*. It is used:

a) in its primary sense.

คุณมีเงินบ้างไหม

Do you have any money?

b) as the equivalent of the phrase *there is/are*.

มีคอรัปชั่นมากในประเทศไทย

There is a great deal of corruption in Thailand.

มีคนถามว่า

There was one person who asked...

เมื่อ

A noun meaning *time*. It is used:

a) in its literal sense.

ในเมื่อเกิดมีเหตุการณ์ร้ายแรง

In the event of an emergency...

b) as the relative adverb *when*.

เมื่อนักข่าวเราได้เรียนถามท่านอธิบดีว่า

When our reporters asked the chairman

c) it precedes some time phrase with reference to the past.

เมื่อปีที่แล้ว

Last year...

เมื่อเดือนก่อน

Last month...

d) when followed by **ไร** it denotes the interrogative pronoun *when.*

เขามาเมื่อไร

When did he come?

คุณจะปราศรัยทางวิทยุครั้งใหม่เมื่อไรครับ

When are you going to make another radio broadcast?

แม้

A conjunction variously translated as *although, regardless of, whether.* It is also used as an adverb meaning *even.*

แม้คุณจะเซ็นอะไรลงไปมันก็จะไม่ช่วยให้คุณดีขึ้น

Regardless of what you sign, it won't help you.

แม้ว่ายังไม่มีข่าวว่ามีเหตุการณ์รุนแรงเกิดขึ้น

Although there has not yet been any reports of violence...

แม้ประชาชนจะต้องการหรือไม่ก็ตาม

Whether the people want it or not...

แม้ในประเทศที่ไกลแสนไกล

Even in countries which are very far away...

ไม่

A negative particle which negates all forms of the verb except the imperative (**อย่า**). Don't forget that the concept of verb is broader in Thai than in English.

ผมบอกไม่ได้

I can't say.

ไม่น้อยกว่าสิบคนได้บอกเรื่องนี้กับผม

No less than ten people have told me that.

กติกาสัญญาไม่รุกรานกัน

A non-aggression pact...

ย่อม (จะ)

An auxiliary denoting the probability or likeliness of the following verb.

คณะกรรมการย่อมทราบอยู่แล้วว่า

The commission is probably aware...

เขาย่อมจะทำงานได้ผลกว่าคนอื่น

He is likely to get better results in his work than anyone else.

ยัง

An adverb meaning *still* or *yet*. Note the idiomatic use in the last example.

เรายังมีเวลาอีกมากนัก

We still have plenty of time.

รัฐบาลยังไม่ได้ตกลงใจ

The government has not yet agreed.

เขาตอบมาหรือยัง ยังครับ

Has he replied yet? Not yet.

ยัง

A preposition denoting motion towards a person or object.

ผมได้ส่งจดหมายไปยังประธานาธิบดี

I sent a letter to the president.

เขาหนีไปยังเมืองจีน

He fled to China.

ยิ่ง

An adverb meaning *increasingly, extremely*. It is used:

    a) in its primary sense.

เขารู้สึกไม่พอใจยิ่งขึ้น

He felt more and more displeased.

    b) with to form the comparative.

สำคัญยิ่งกว่านี้รายงานนั้นได้ส่งไปยังรัฐมนตรี

More important than that, the report was sent to the minister.

    c) as a coordinating particle to form the patter *the ...-er, the*   *...-er.*

ยิ่งพูดเสียงของเขายิ่งดัง

The more he spoke, the louder his voice became.

ยิ่งเร็วก็ยิ่งดี

The sooner, the better.

รวม

A verb meaning *to join, put together*. It is combined with ทั้ง to mean *including* and with ทั้งหมด to mean *all-inclusive*.

ประเทศต่างๆรวมทั้งมาลาเซีย

Various nations, including Malaysia...

พลเมืองรวมทั้งหมดมีจำนวน 15 ล้านคน

The total population is fifteen million.

ร่วม

A verb meaning *to join with, share*. ร่วมกับ means *with* (in the sense of physical accompaniment), while ร่วมกัน means *together*. This is a good example of the difference between กับ and กัน.

เขาทำงานในโรงงานเคมีร่วมกับผม

He works with me at the chemical factory.

เขาและผมได้ทำงานร่วมกัน

He and I worked together.

ระหว่าง

A preposition meaning *between, among*. It is used:

a) in its primary sense.

ถ้าเกิดมีสงครามขึ้นในระหว่างสองประเทศนี้ แล้วจะต้องมีสงครามทั่วไปขึ้นในระหว่างชาติ ทั้งหลาย

If there is a war between the two countries, there will be a general war among nations.

การค้าขายระหว่างประเทศชะงัก

International trade...

b) in time phrases to mean *during*.

ระหว่างฤดูฝน

During the rainy season...

ระหว่างเป็นประธานาธิบดีสมัยแรก

During his first term as president...

ราว

An adverb meaning *about* or *approximately*.

ผมคอยอยู่ราวสิบนาที

I waited about 10 minutes.

บ้านนี้มีราคาราว 1 แสนบาท

The cost of this house is about 100000 baht.

เรา

The first person plural pronoun (*we, us*). This is the only explicitly plural pronoun in the Thai language.

เราเป็นคนตั้งคำถาม

We are the people who ask the questions.

ผู้สื่อข่าวพิเศษของเรา

Our special correspondent.

เรื่อง

A noun meaning *story, account, matter*. It is often best translated as *about*.

ผมได้คิดถึงเรื่องนี้อยู่มาก

I have been thinking a lot about this (matter).

เราจะไม่ลงเรื่องนี้

We won't publish this story.

ผมไม่ชอบพูดเรื่องการเมือง

I don't like to talk about politics.

ลง

A verb meaning *to descend, go down*. It is used:

a) in its primary sense.

ผมลงจากม้า

I got down from the horse.

b) as a secondary verb indicating motion downwards, either literally or figuratively. It may be translated as *down* or, more often, left untranslated.

เมื่อผมกลับมาถึงกรุงเทพฯสงครามในยุโรปสิ้น

สุดลงแล้ว

When I returned to Bangkok, the war in Europe had already ended.

เครื่องบินพม่าได้ทำการทิ้งระเบิดลงในหมู่บ้าน

ไทยจังหวัดแม่ฮ่องสอน

Burmese aeroplanes bombed a Thai village in Mae Hong Son.

เขานั่งลง

He sat down.

ละ

A particle meaning *a* or *per*. Care should be taken because the word order is the opposite to English, this can lead to a very different word order throughout the entire sentence. When preceded by **แต่** it means *each*.

เขาอ่านหนังสือคืนละสามเล่ม

He reads three books a night.

เครื่องบินสัปดาห์ละ 6 ลำ

Six planes a week...

เราแบ่งกันออกเป็นหมู่ๆละสิบสองคน

We split up into groups of 12.

กระทรวงแต่ละกระทรวง

Each ministry...

เลย

An intensifying particle which is used in many different circumstances. The more common are:

a) as a final particle after a negative verb.

ผมไม่มีเงินเลย

I have no money at all.

เขามิได้ให้เหตุผลอย่างใดเลย

He didn't give any reason at all.

ผมไม่ได้พูดอะไรเลย

I didn't say anything at all.

b) to intensify an imperative.

ไปเลย

Just go!

c) at the beginning of a clause meaning *then, thereupon*.

เขาถูกจับไปทำงานในค่ายกักกันแล้ว เลยถูกส่ง ไปภาคใต้

He was captured and obliged to work in a forced labour camp. He was then sent to the south.

แล้ว

An adverb meaning *already*. Due to the lack of explicit tense markers in Thai, this is very commonly used to mark the past tense. It is used:

a) in this primary meaning.

เราเสียเวลามามากแล้ว

We have (already) wasted a great deal of time.

ผมแน่ใจว่าเขารู้แล้ว

I was certain that he already knew.

b) as the initial word of a clause meaning *then, afterwards*.

แล้วคุณจะทำอย่างไรได้

Then what will you be able to do?

c) as a part of some time phrases.

เมื่อปีที่แล้ว

Last year...

d) in certain set expressions.

แล้วแต่คุณ

It depends on you.

ดีแล้ว

That's good.

และ

The conjunction *and,* used to connect nouns and clauses. In speech in is often extended to **และก็**

ข้าราชการและนักการเมือง
Government officials and politicians

การค้าและการพาณิชย์
Trade and commerce

ผมเข้าใจและขอบคุณมาก
I understand and I thank you very much.

ขอเบียร์ขวดหนึ่งแล้วก็เป๊ปซี่ขวดหนึ่งครับ
I'd like a beer and one Pepsi.

ว่า

A verb meaning *to say, declare*. It is used:

a) in its primary sense.

เขานิ่งอยู่นานแล้วว่า
He was silent for a long time and then said...

b) to introduce secondary clauses after verbs of speaking, thinking, perceiving etc. This is most often translated as *that* but many different translations are possible, and obvious, from context.

รายงานข่าวแจ้งว่า
A report states that...

ผมไม่รู้ว่าเขาจะมาที่นี่หรือไม่
I don't know whether he will come here or not.

อีกส่วนหนึ่งเรียกว่าเขตบี

The other part is called Zone B.

c) in certain set phrases to mean *to be concerned with*.

รัฐมนตรีว่าการต่างประเทศ

Foreign minister.

เว้น

A verb meaning *to omit*. It is commonly used with **แต่** :

a) as a preposition meaning *except*.

ทุกๆคนไปเว้นแต่ผม

Everyone went except me.

b) as a subordinating conjunction meaning *unless*.

อิสรภาพที่ผมได้นั้นคงไม่มีอยู่นานนักเว้นแต่ผม
จะยอมตกเป็นเครื่องมือของพวก

The freedom which I have obtained will not last long unless I permit myself to become a tool of the party.

ผมจะไม่ไปเว้นแต่ผมจะได้รับข่าวจากคุณ

I won't go unless I hear from you.

ไว้

A verb meaning *to keep, preserve*. Its main use is as a secondary verb denoting continuance or as the equivalent to the adverb *behind*. It is often left untranslated.

คุณจับสามีฉันไว้ทำไม

Why did you arrest my husband?

เขาได้เก็บเงินไว้ได้บ้าง

He was able to save some money.

เขาได้บันทึกสิ่งทุกอย่างไว้ละเอียด

He noted down everything in detail.

ส่วน

A noun meaning *part*. It is more commonly used as a preposition meaning *as for, regarding*.

ส่วนหนึ่งของเรื่องนี้เป็นจริง

A part of this is true.

ส่วนผมนั้นคุณไม่ต้องเป็นห่วง

As for me, you don't need to worry.

ส่วนการที่

Regarding the fact that...

สัก

An adverb used to emphasise the paucity of the expression it follows. It is often translated as *just, even*.

โปรดรอสักครู่ครับ

Wait just a little while, please.

ไม่มีใครสักคนเดียวตลอดทั้งถนน

There is not even a single person along the whole road.

ผมอยากขอคุณสักอย่างหนึ่ง

I just want to make one request.

สำหรับ

A preposition which corresponds to the many uses of English *for*. It is slightly bookish and it some instances it is replaced by ให้ in the spoken language.

รัฐบาลใหม่สำหรับประเทศไทย

A new government for Thailand...

จังหวะอันเหมาะสมสำหรับการโฆษณา

A suitable time for propaganda.

สิ่ง

A noun meaning *thing*. Also used as a classifier.

สิ่งใดที่ฉันต้องการแล้วเป็นได้ทุกอย่าง

Anything that I wanted I got.

ทุกสิ่งทุกอย่างเรียบร้อย

Everything is ready.

สิ่งใดสิ่งหนึ่ง

Anything; any one among many.

สุด

An adjective meaning *to be extreme, ultimate*. Used mostly in the form **ที่สุด** to form the superlative. The phrase **ในที่สุด** is also common, it means *finally, ultimately*.

เพื่อนดีที่สุดของเขาคนหนึ่ง

One of his best friends...

คุณอยู่ในอันตรายอย่างที่สุด

You are in the utmost danger.

ในสุดเขาก็ถูกขับออกจากพรรค

He was finally expelled from the party.

สู่

A preposition denoting motion towards an object. It can be translated as *to, on* or *into* depending on context.

ตำรวจกลับมาสู่จังหวัด

The police returned to the province.

เราสามคนได้เดินทางไปสู่เกาะสมุย

The three of us travelled to Koh Samui.

ลูกระเบิดตกสู่ค่ายทหารหลายแห่ง

The bombs fell on several military encampments.

เสร็จ

A verb meaning *to finish*. It is mainly used as a secondary verb to indicate completion of the main verb.

เมื่อกินเสร็จแล้วเขาก็ลุกขึ้นจากโต๊ะ

When he had finished eating he got up from the table.

นายกรัฐมนตรีใหม่ได้จัดตั้งคณะรัฐมนตรีเสร็จแล้ว

The new premier has completed the formation of his new cabinet.

พอพูดเสร็จเขาก็จากไป

As soon as he finished speaking he left.

เสีย

A verb with many meaning including *to lose, fail, spend (time or money)*. It is used:

a) in its primary sense.

ผมได้รู้ว่าเขาเสียชีวิตเสียแล้วจากภัยทาง

อากาศ

I learned that he lost his life in an air raid.

b) as an emphatic particle, which is often untranslated.

อย่าลืมข้อความนี้เสีย

Don't forget this fact.

ผมไม่มีอำนาจอะไรเสียเลย

I don't have any authority at all.

จงทำลายจดหมายนี้เสีย

Destroy this letter.

c) in the compound **เสียใจ**.

ผมเสียใจที่จะกล่าวว่า

I regret to say that...

หน้า

A noun meaning *face* or *page*. It is also used in some spatial and temporal relationships with the meaning of *in front of; next*.

เราไม่กล้ามองหน้ากันเอง

We didn't dare look at each other (at each other's face.)

ผมได้มาหยุดยืนหน้าบ้าน

I stopped in front of the house.

ในแนวหน้าการรบ

In the front line of the battle...

เขาจะได้เจรจาขอซื้อสำหรับปีหน้า

He will discuss purchases for next year.

หมด

A verb meaning *to be used up, finished*. It is used:

a) in its primary sense.

เขาต้องออกเพราะเงินหมดแล้ว

He had to leave because his money ran out.

b) as a secondary verb indicating completion or exhaustion.

เราจะคอยอยู่จนกว่าทหารจีนออกไปหมด

We'll wait until the Chinese troops have all left.

c) in the compound **ทั้งหมด**, meaning *all (together)*. For examples see: **ทั้ง**

หรือ

A coordinating conjunction meaning *or* used to link either nouns or clauses. It is used:

a) in its primary sense.

ผมไม่รู้ว่าเขาจะมาที่นี่หรือไม่

I don't know whether he will come here or not.

สี่หรือห้าครั้ง

Four or five times...

b) as an interrogative particle, most often at the end of the sentence to hint at a positive answer. It may be moved so that it follows an emphasised word.

แน่ใจหรือ

Are you sure? (expecting the answer: yes)

นี่หรือหนังสือพิมพ์ที่คุณอ่าน

Are these the newspapers that you read?

หลัง

A noun meaning *back (of the body)*. It is also used:

a) as the preposition *behind*.

หลังประตู

Behind the door...

b) when followed by **จาก** as the conjunction *after*.

หลังจากเขาได้ตายไปแล้วสองสามปี

After he had been dead for two or three years.

c) in the phrase **หลังที่สุด** meaning *final, last*.

เขาเป็นคนหลังที่สุดที่ถูกปรึกษา

He was the last to be consulted.

หลาย

A quantifier meaning *several* or *many*. It is usually used with a classifier. It can be reduplicated for emphasis.

เราคุยกันหลายชั่วโมง

We talked together for several hours.

มีพวกที่ร่วมไปกันผมหลายคน

There were several people co-operating with me.

เขามาที่นี่หลายๆครั้ง

He came here many times.

หาก

A conjunction meaning *if* or *but*. It also occurs in the forms **ถ้าหาก**

and **หากว่า** with no change of meaning.

หากผมจำไม่ผิด

If I remember rightly...

ถ้าหากมีเหตุฉุกเฉินเขาจะได้ปฏิบัติการทันที

If there is an emergency, they will be able to go into action immediately.

เขาไม่เพียงแต่มีสิทธิหากมีหน้าที่ที่จะหารือกันเรา

He has not only the right, but the duty to consult with us.

เหมือน

An adjective meaning *to be similar, the same*. It is used:

a) in its primary sense, often followed by **กับ/กัน.**

ฐานะของเขาไม่เหมือนกับคนนอกพรรค

Their status is not similar to that of those who are outside of   the party.

b) as the preposition *like*.

คุณพูดเหมือนเด็กๆ

You speak like a child.

c) in the phrase **เหมือนกัน** meaning *also, too*.

ผมก็ดีใจเหมือนกัน

I'm pleased too.

เหล่า

A noun meaning *group*. Its main use is as a classifier with this meaning, often used to indicate the plural – even of uncountable nouns (see the third example).

นายทหารเหล่านี้

These officers...

คุณต้องไปดูสิ่งเหล่านี้ทั้งหมด

You must go and see all these things.

เธอได้เงินเหล่านี้มาจากไหน

Where did you get all of this money?

แห่ง

A noun meaning *place*. It is also used:

a) as a sign of a possessive relationship, especially where the "possessor" is a country or region.

การรถไฟแห่งประเทศไทย

Thai State Railways

b) as a classifier for places and locations.

ค่ายหลายแห่ง

Several camps...

พวกนักเรียนในสถาบันแห่งนี้

The students in this institute...

ให้

A verb meaning *to give*. It is used:

a) in its primary sense.

ผมอยากให้คำแนะนำแก่คุณสักหน่อย

I would like to give you a word of advice.

b) as a preposition meaning *for, to, on behalf of*.

ฉันเป็นนักสืบให้คุณไม่ได้

I can't be a spy for you.

ผมหยิบหนังสือเดินทางส่งให้เขา

I picked up my passport and handed it over to him.

c) as a verb meaning *to let, allow,* or *to make someone do something*.

ให้เขานั่งลงเสียก่อนเถอะ

Have him sit down first.

ให้เขาทำตามใจเขา

Let him do what he wants.

d) following a verb of desire when the subject wishes someone else to do something. It is optional and can be   thought of as meaning *to cause, induce, effect*.

ผมไม่อยากให้เขาไปกับผม

I don't want them to go with me.

ผมต้องการให้คุณทั้งสามคนไปที่นั่น

I want all three of you to go there.

ไหน

An interrogative adjective meaning *which* or *what.* It can be used in place of virtually any interrogative word.

ผมไม่รู้ว่าจะไปทางไหน

I don't know which way to go.

คุณต้องการพบคนไหนล่ะครับ

Which person do you want to meet?

เขาถามผมว่าจะไปไหน

He asked me where I was going

เดี๋ยวนี้สามีเธออยู่ที่ไหน

Where is your husband?

ไหม

An interrogative particle, it converts any sentence into a yes/no question. It is placed at the end of the relevant clause, although in speech many particles can follow it.

ผมจะถูกยิงไหม

Will I be shot?

คุณพูดภาษาอังกฤษเป็นไหม

Can you speak English?

คุณเคยนึกบ้างไหมว่าสหรัฐอเมริกาเป็นอย่างไร

Have you ever wondered what the USA is like?

อย่า

A particle used to form the negative imperative. It is often softened by adding **นะ** at the end of the sentence.

อย่ากลัวนะ
Don't be afraid.

อย่าทำอะไรโง่ๆ
Don't do anything foolish.

อย่าออกไปเลย
Don't leave.

อย่าง

A noun meaning *way, manner*. It has a variety of additional uses such as:

a) to form adverbs.

เขาพูดถึงเรื่องนี้อย่างมีความรู้
He discussed the subject learnedly.

อย่าพูดอย่างนั้น
Don't speak like that.

ถ้าผมถูกจับก็คงถูกยิงทิ้งอย่างไม่
If I am caught I will unquestionably be shot.

b) to mean *kind* or *type*.

ผมเคยได้ยินเรื่องอย่างนี้

I used to hear things like this (of this type).

c) to mean *thing* in the phrase **ทุกๆอย่าง**, *everything*.

ผมยินดีที่จะทำทุกๆอย่างที่ผมทำได้

I shall be glad to do everything I can.

d) in the phrase **อย่างไร** meaning *how, what sort of*.

เขาเป็นคนอย่างไร

What sort of person is he?

ผมไม่ทราบว่าจะตอบคำถามข้อนี้ได้อย่างไร

I didn't know how I would answer this question.

อย่างไรก็ดี

In any event...

e) in the compound **อย่างใด** meaning *at all*.

ผมไม่เห็นว่าจะเป็นอันตรายแต่อย่างใด

I didn't think it would be at all dangerous.

อยู่

A verb meaning *to be located*. It is used:

a) in its primary meaning.

ผมเชื่อว่าเขาอยู่ในบ้าน

I think that he is in the house.

b) as a verb meaning *to live, reside*.

คุณอยู่ที่ไหน

Where do you live?

c) as a secondary verb to show that the action is continuing. It is often used with **กำลัง**.

เขากำลังตรวจดูเอกสารต่างๆอยู่

He was examining various documents.

เขานิ่งอยู่นาน

He was silent for a long time.

ออก

A verb meaning *to go out, leave, issue*. It is used:

a) in it primary sense.

ผมออกบ้านตรงไปยังกองบัญชาการตำรวจ

I left the house and went directly to Police Headquarters.

เขาได้ออกคำสั่งขัดแย้ง

He issued contradictory orders.

b) as a secondary verb indicating motion outwards.

ในที่สุดเขาถูกขับออกจากพรรค

He was finally driven out of the party.

ผมมองออกไปทางหน้าต่าง

I looked out of the window.

อะไร

The interrogative pronoun *what*. It is a very common word used:

a) its primary sense.

นั่นอะไร

What is that?

ผมไม่รู้ว่าคุณพูดอะไร

I don't know what you are saying?

b) as an indefinite pronoun, *something, anything, any.*

คุณคิดว่าจะเกิดอะไรอีกบ้างไหม

Do you think anything else will happen?

เขาไม่ได้ทำอะไรผิดเลย

He hasn't committed any violation.

อัน

A relative pronoun meaning *which* or *that*. It is extremely bookish and for the foreign learner only passive recognition of this word is necessary.

การอุตสาหกรรมของประเทศอันเป็นหลักสำคัญใน

การเศรษฐกิจ

The industry of the nation, which is an important aspect of the economy.

ในอนาคตอันใกล้นี้

In the near future...

อาจ(จะ)

A pre-verbal auxiliary denoting possibility.

คนบางคนอาจจะไม่เห็นพ้องด้วยกับคุณ

Some people may not agree with you.

เขาอาจหนีรอดไปได้

He may have been able to escape.

บางทีเขาอาจจะมา

Perhaps he will come.

อีก

An adverb meaning *more, in addition, again*.

ผมไม่มีอะไรจะพูดอีก

I have nothing more to say.

เราได้สัญญากันว่าจะพบกันอีก

We promised each other that we would meet again.

ผู้ชายอีกคนหนึ่ง

Another man...

อื่น

An adjective meaning *another, different*.

เรายังมีหนทางอื่นอีก

We have other means.

เขาไม่มีที่อื่นที่จะไป

He has no other place to go.

ไม่มีใครอื่นนอกจากคุณที่จะทำการนี้ได้

Nobody other than you could do it.

ผมจะทำอย่างอื่นไม่ได้

I could not have acted otherwise.

เอง

An emphatic pronoun translated as ~*self*. It is used:

a) in its primary sense.

ผมเองก็รู้สึกอย่างเดียวกัน

I myself felt the same way.

ประธานาธิบดีเองต้องรับผิดชอบต่อชาติ

The president himself is responsible for the nation.

b) an intensifying particle translated as *just, very* or left untranslated.

ในขณะเดียวกันนั้นเองการตระเตรียมเพื่อสงคราม ก็ได้เริ่มต้นขึ้น

At that very same time preparations for war begun.

คณะกรรมการโรงงานเพิ่งเสร็จประชุมเดี๋ยวนี้ เอง

The factory committee has just now concluded its meeting.

Below are five newspaper style editorials along with their translation. These are here for you to see how frequent some of these words are and how they can be translated in idiomatic English.

สืบเนื่องจากเหตุการณ์ระเบิดที่หน้าห้างสรรพสินค้าสยามพารากอนเมื่อเย็น วันอาทิตย์ที่ผ่านมา ทำให้ตระหนักได้ว่ายังคงมีคลื่นใต้น้ำที่คอยก่อความวุ่นวาย ตำรวจยังไม่ทราบถึงแรงจูงใจที่แน่ชัดในการก่อความไม่สงบในครั้งนี้ แต่ สันนิษฐานได้ว่าเป็นการสร้างสถานการณ์ เพื่อต้องการทำให้ผู้คนตื่นกลัวเพื่อจะ ลดความน่าเชื่อถือในการบริหารประเทศของรัฐบาล ภายใต้การนำของพลเอก ประยุทธ์ จันโอชา จึงนับได้ว่าเป็นงานหนักของรัฐบาลชุดนี้ ที่ต้องรักษาความสงบเรียบร้อยภายในประเทศ เปรียบเหมือนการรับศึกหลาย ๆ ด้านพร้อม ๆ กันทีเดียว

After the bomb explosion in front of Siam Paragon shopping mall last Sunday evening it has become clear that there is still an undercurrent of a violent uprising. Police still not 100% sure about the criminal motivation behind this explosion. But the police theory is that is was designed to inconvenience the public and make people feel insecure in order to discredit the government under the leadership of Gen. Prayuth Chan-ocha. It is a difficult task for the government to maintain peace and order in Thailand at this time as there as this is one of a number of ongoing crises.

สัตย์เป็นประเด็นที่คนไทยให้ความสำคัญอยู่เสมอ จะเห็นได้ จากความพยายามผลักดันให้มีพระราชบัญญัติคุ้มครองสัตว์ภาค ประชาชนออกมา เนื่องจากทุกวันนี้ประเทศไทยมีกฎหมายที่อ่อนมาก ในการดูแลสัตว์และเจ้าหน้าที่ก็ไม่เคยใส่ใจ คนไทยที่รักสัตว์ทั้งหลาย ไม่ต้องการแบบนั้นอีกแล้ว จึงมีการผลักดัน ร่าง พรบ.คุ้มครองสัตว์ฯ ฉบับภาคประชาชนให้มีผลบังคับใช้อย่างเต็มที่ เพราะนี่เป็นโอกาส สุดท้ายที่เราจะมีกลไกทางกฎหมายที่เข้มแข็งเพื่อมาดูแลสัตว์

Animal trafficking has become an important issue for Thai people. You can tell from the efforts in the public sector to introduce an animal protection act. Due to the current weak laws the officials are powerless. Thai people who are generally animal lovers don't want to be like this any more. So there are movements to make the public sector animal protection act draft become fully effective fully. Because this is the last chance to have a strong animal protection law mechanism.

สิ่งที่ทุกคนปรารถนา คือ ชีวิตที่มีแต่ความสุขและ
ร่ำรวยเงินทอง แต่ในชีวิตความเป็นจริงของ คนส่วน
ใหญ่ ช่างสวนทางกับความปรารถนาของพวกเขา
เหลือเกิน เป็นความจริงที่เงินไม่ใช่ สิ่งที่สำคัญที่สุด
แต่สิ่งที่ผลักดันให้คนทำสิ่งต่าง ๆ ก็เพราะความ
ต้องการเงินนั่นเอง การลักเล็ก ขโมยน้อย การฉกชิง
วิ่งราว การปล้นจี้ จึงมีให้เห็นอยู่ทั่วไปตามหน้า
หนังสือพิมพ์ การเสพข่าวอย่างนี้ดูเหมือน จะกลายเป็น
เรื่องปกติไปเสียแล้วสำหรับคนในสมัยปัจจุบัน

Everyone wants to have a happy life and to be rich. But the reality for
most people is totally opposite. It's true that money is not the most
important thing but the lack of money is what drives most human
activities. Therefore, in general, we see stories about stealing, looting
and robbery in the newspapers day after day. It has now become the
norm to see these types of stories on the front page everyday.

หลังการลงมติของสนช.ถอดถอน น.ส.ยิ่งลักษณ์ ชิน
วัตร อดีตนายกรัฐมนตรีด้วยคะแนนท่วมท้น 190
คะแนน ส่งผลให้ น.ส.ยิ่งลักษณ์ ถูกตัดสิทธิ์ทางการ
เมือง 5 ปีตามกฎหมาย ทำให้หลายคนตั้ง คำถามว่า
จะเกิดอะไรขึ้นต่อไปข้างหน้าจากผลของมติครั้งนี้ จะ
เกิดความวุ่นวาย ความรุนแรง ใน ลักษณะของ
การเมืองนอกสภาขึ้นมาอีกหรือไม่? แต่เนื่องด้วยตอน
นี้ประเทศไทยยังอยู่ภายใต้ กฎอัยการศึกอยู่ ดังนั้น
การก่อเหตุในทำนองนี้จึงไม่ง่ายนัก ส่วนประเด็นที่น่า
สนใจ และต้อง ขบคิดว่าจะหาทางออกอย่างไรหลัง
จากนี้ ก็คือ ประเทศไทยจะผ่านพ้นความขัดแย้ง
ทางการเมืองที่ มีมาก่อนหน้านี้ได้หรือไม่ หรือ ไป สู่
สังคม ที่ อยู่กันได้ แม้มี ความเห็นต่าง และ ต่อสู้
ทางการเมือง ไปตามระบอบ ได้หรือไม่

After the NLA (National Legislative Assembly) voted
overwhelmingly by a majority of 190 to remove Yingluck Shinawatra
the Thailand former prime minister from her post. As a result Yingluck
has also been banned from Thai politics for 5 years. People have
questioned what happen after this vote. Will there be disorder, violence
and further pursuit of Shinawatra's family? But because Thailand is
still under martial law it will not easy to do any of these. The
interesting issue and what we have to pay attention to is how can
Thailand leave previous political conflicts behind? How can we live
together in harmony even though there are differences in opinion? Can
we have a fair political system?

สืบเนื่องจากที่ตำรวจเปิดแถลงข่าวว่า สามารถจับตัว
คนร้ายที่ฆาตกรรมนักท่องเที่ยว 2 คน บน เกาะเต่าได้
แล้ว ผู้ต้องหาเป็นชายชาวพม่า 2 คนที่ทำงานเป็น
ลูกจ้างในร้านอาหารแห่งหนึ่ง ใกล้ กับสถานที่เกิดเหตุ
ด้วยเหตุนี้ทำให้นายรัษฎา มนูรัษฎา ทนายความ
อาวุโส และทีมทนายความ จากสำนักงานสิทธิมนุษย
ชน สภาทนายความ ต้องใช้เวลาสอบปากคำผู้ต้องหา
นาน 5 ชั่วโมง ก่อนที่จะเปิดเผยว่า ผู้ต้องหาได้กลับ
คำให้การ และต้องการร้องขอความเป็นธรรม เนื่องจาก
ถูก ทำร้ายเพื่อให้ยอมรับสารภาพ ประเด็นนี้จึงกลาย
เป็นที่จับตามองของสังคมอีกครั้งหนึ่งว่า ในที่สุดแล้ว
ทั้ง 2 คนนี้จะกลายเป็น แพะรับบาป อีกหรือไม่

According to the police statement, the two men accused of murdering
two tourists on Koh Tao are two Burmese men who work in a
restaurant near the scene of the incident. After this Mr. Ratsadaa
Manuratsadaa, a senior lawyer and other lawyers from the office of
Human Rights spent five hours with the accused After this
Mr.Ratsadaa said the accused want to retract their statement and would
like to get justification because they were beaten in order to produce a
confession. This has become a hot issue for people again as to whether
these two men are guilty or just scapegoats?

Also available from JiaHu Books

A Burmese Reader - Annotated Selections from the
Sudhammacari 978-1-909669-08-6

Fundamenta Krestomatio 978-1-909669-03-1

Beowulf: Text And Glossary 978-1-909669-43-7